HELP THEM UP

Praise for *Help Them Up*

"In today's climate, and perhaps more than ever, we are confronted with the fact that sports and teams are so much more than just X's and O's. Dan's book does an excellent job of articulating the importance of relationships and servant leadership that are paramount to the success of any team. Dan's insight into team-building and culture, and his unique way of presenting strategies for building both, make this book an invaluable tool for coaches at any level."

—Brooke Wyckoff
Florida State University, Women's Basketball Associate Head Coach

"Relentless. Relentless is probably the best word I can use to describe Dan Horwitz. Dan is incredibly hardworking with a focus on improvement. In his latest work, he takes a very unique approach to the game of basketball in a way that is easy to understand and relate to. For those that have wondered how to team-build or struggled to understand some of the little things that help to build a champion, this book is for you."

—James Jones
Yale University, Men's Basketball Head Coach

"Dan has an incredible passion for the game of basketball, but his drive and commitment to help serve others is what I admire the most. Dan offers a unique perspective on team-building and creating a championship-winning culture. This is a must-read for all coaches and players who embrace all the little things that help build champions both on and off the court."

—Mike Donnelly
Florida Southern, Men's Basketball Head Coach

"I've known Dan for quite some time, and I don't know anyone who is more passionate for both basketball and helping others. I absolutely love this book and all it provides for both coaches and players! I'm so excited to implement these principles with my youth team and provide them all the tools they need to succeed!"

—Sarah Hope
Boston University, Former Women's Basketball Student-Athlete and Assistant Coach

"I hadn't met anyone so determined to learn and become the best person and coach they can be until I met Dan. Not many people see basketball for more than just the skill and talent it takes to win championships. It takes a special person to transform what it means to be a team player. Dan not only embodies these little things in his everyday life, but he lays them out perfectly in this book with examples and interactive sections for coaches and players to learn what it really takes to be a champion."

—Erica DeCandido
Tufts University Class of 2020
Women's Basketball Student-Athlete
2020 D3 National Player of the Year

"Success starts with relationships and Dan does a great job at emphasizing the importance of connection as the foundation to building these relationships. In *Help Them Up*, athletes and coaches are provided simple yet effective strategies and exercises to assist them in creating a strength that is more important than talent alone. While the book is geared toward basketball, it is easily applicable to other sports and life as well."

—Tami Matheny
Mental Game Coach and Author of The Confident Athlete *and* This Is Good: A Journey to Overcoming Adversity

HELP THEM UP

14 PRINCIPLES TO EDUCATE ENERGIZE AND EMPOWER YOUR TEAM TO BUILD A CHAMPIONSHIP CULTURE

DAN HORWITZ

The information in this book is meant to supplement, not replace, proper basketball training. Like any sport involving speed, balance, and environmental factors, basketball poses some inherent risk. The author advises readers to take full responsibility for their safety and to know their limits. Do not take risks beyond your level of experience, aptitude, training, and comfort level.

ISBN: - Paperback
eISBN: - ePub
eISBN: - mobi

Printed in the United States of America 1 0 0 2 2 0

♾This paper meets the requirements of ANSI/NISO Z39.48-1992 (Permanence of Paper)

Cover by Abdo_96 at 99designs

DISCLAIMER

The following information is all from the author's personal experiences, observations in person and on film, and speaking with teams featured in the book. All of the information is based on an outside perspective and does not reflect information directly related to these teams.

DEDICATION

This book is dedicated to my dad,

Richard Horwitz.

He unexpectedly passed away shortly after my twenty-first birthday at the age of sixty-three. He loved to read books, and it makes me happy knowing he would have enjoyed reading this one.

For twenty-one years, my dad gave my siblings and me unconditional love. He taught me to enjoy life, work hard, have fun, laugh, smile, and the five-second rule: If you drop food on the ground, it's still fine to eat it if you pick it up fast enough! He traveled all over New England to support and watch me play the game of basketball. He was always in the stands cheering my team on, regardless if I was playing or coaching, and always had something positive to say after the game. He lived life to the fullest, could spark a conversation with anyone, and enjoyed dancing. I hope to share my dad's love for putting his team first; his family and his friends, with as many people as I possibly can. Every day is so precious, and his positive outlook on life was contagious to everyone around him.

I love you, Dad.

CONTENTS

INTRODUCTION

> *Nobody cares how much you know, until they know how much you care.*
> ***—Theodore Roosevelt***

I truly love the process of building teams and it's my hope that this book will assist in helping others improve their teams! Thank you for taking the time to read this. Thank you for making a difference in the lives of others.

Why I Wrote This Book

Time is precious. Most basketball seasons begin with a limited amount of preparation time before the first scrimmage and game. In a day, we only have 1,440 minutes. In a two-hour practice, we only have 120 minutes.

It was eye-opening when I began watching games in person and through film study. There were a lot of similar and consistent behaviors the best teams used. Every second matters, and every second adds up until the final buzzer goes off. The best teams understand this and maximize their time together.

What if I told you fourteen principles exist that lead to stronger team cohesion, trust, selflessness, loyalty, and joy? What if I told you these principles can be successfully implemented within the limited time you have with your team?

These principles require no talent at all, just knowledge, intention, persistence, and commitment.

My mission is to help as many people as possible have a great basketball experience with the limited time you have together as a team. This book will help you learn and validate the qualities of what it takes to be a transformational coach and teammate, and will empower you to take accountability. Through learning and practicing the fourteen principles outlined here, you will have the opportunity to create relationships and memories that will last a lifetime.

I hope you learn to measure success in a different way than the scoreboard. As athletes and coaches, we play the game with the intention to win—something that is not fully in our control.

If you are a coach reading this book, I challenge you to ask every member of the team these important questions at the end of the season to measure your team's success. If you are a player, evaluate teams you have played on and answer these questions. If you're not satisfied with your answers, we will do our best to improve your experience for your next team with the principles in this book.

- Did you have fun?
- Did you try your best?
- Did we improve as individuals and as a team?
- Did we challenge each other?
- Did we make each other better?
- Did we create a safe, enjoyable, and hardworking environment?
- Did you feel valued?
- Did you feel empowered to speak up, use your voice, and take ownership of your team?
- Did you learn life lessons that you think will serve you well in life, outside of basketball?

If the answer to these questions is yes, the team had a successful season.

I want you, the reader, to know that I have your back. It's my mission, by the end of this book, to have you feeling prepared to take your leadership skills to the next level. The team-first mentality is when a team finds ways to contribute and benefit the group through their words and actions. When a team buys into the team-first mentality, amazing things can happen!

It would be naive to ignore the fact that there is a talent aspect to winning games. However, when players and coaches genuinely enjoy the journey, the final result doesn't define the season; the experience does.

What This Book Can Do for You

I want every person who finishes this book to feel empowered and confident to be a leader within their teams. In order to build a championship culture, you need the tools to do so. This book will provide you with an inside look at some of the most successful NCAA men's and women's basketball programs, two high-school teams, and a middle-school travel team. All of these teams have one thing in common: an emphasis on building consistent habits that lead to a championship culture.

Building and enhancing a team's culture will not prevent adversity from occurring. However, it will prepare teams to feel more confident, resilient, and fully equipped to embrace the challenge—collectively!

This book will add value to players and coaches who want to create a championship culture and enhance their team's leadership skills. The fourteen principles outlined in these pages can be worked on in practices, games, and off the court. Although basketball is the sport I used for my examples, I believe all team sports can incorporate these principles. I will share all I know to help you feel prepared to take action!

Many life lessons can be taught using sports as a platform. As a coach, accumulating knowledge on culture and disseminating that knowledge to players can have a long-lasting impact. As a player, you have the ability to maximize your leadership skills, as well as help promote a team environment that will bring out the best in everyone, including yourself.

Showing up every day is the first step to having an impact on your team. Next, bringing a great attitude and positive energy to practice and games will help create an enjoyable and productive environment. Lastly, having a growth mindset—the ability to believe you can learn and improve from every situation—is important in building a championship culture.

About the Author

I have played on losing teams as well as championship teams. Losing is not fun but you can learn a lot more about yourself and your team from a loss than you can from a win. My college-playing career record was 13–87. But ultimately, I am a better person and coach for those experiences, even if it didn't feel like it at the time. The teammates I graduated with deserve a lot of credit for being resilient and mentally tough throughout our college careers. I hope this book will guide your team to an enjoyable and successful season, regardless if you win or lose.

My college-playing and coaching career fueled me to study some of the most successful men's and women's basketball teams in the country. I realized I wanted to be a coach as a sophomore in high school. I took advantage of every opportunity to attend, work, or volunteer at NCAA March Madness regional tournaments, USA basketball youth-development clinics, coaching clinics, college practices, and summer camps. I also had an incredible experience interning for the Syracuse University Men's Basketball program for a summer and learned so much during that experience.

Final Notes

As you begin to read this book, I want to communicate the structure of the chapters.

The fourteen principles start by highlighting a team that executes one of the principles consistently. The "Coaches' Corner: Action Exercise" section is a breakdown for coaches to help implement each principle. The "Players' Perspective" section challenges players reading this book to evaluate themselves by answering the listed questions. It's up to you, the reader, to determine which section applies to you, or if you'd like to read and learn from them all. In basketball, every single member can add value, and this book encourages both players and coaches to work together to build a championship culture.

Interestingly, this book is being released during the COVID-19 pandemic. This has been an emotional and tough time for everyone while trying to figure out our new "normal" lifestyle. The information in this book asks teams to be close to one another in order to execute most of these principles. I want every player and coach to follow safety guidelines and determine which interactions with each other are safe and appropriate. As long as everyone feels comfortable with the way in which their team operates, I believe there are always ways to enhance a team's culture. Like any great team, we will stick together and get through this together!

PRINCIPLE #1

Warm-Up and Stretching

> *Effective teamwork begins and ends with communication.*
> *—Mike Krzyzewski*

The University of Connecticut Women's Basketball team is one of the most accomplished and decorated sport programs in the history of basketball. Geno Auriemma completed his thirty-fifth season as the head coach of the basketball team in 2019–2020. His team set a record by winning 111 games in a row, including two national championships. In 2018, I was fortunate to be able to attend a two-hour practice. Interestingly, the thing that stuck with me the most happened within the first fifteen minutes.

The team's dynamic warm-up was similar to that of a choreographed dance routine. To start, all the players lined up on one sideline, then began traveling from one sideline to the other. Every player was in complete unison with all of their teammates: footwork, the distance covered on the ground, and pace. It was amazing to see.

It became crystal clear to me in that moment that elite teams are intentional with *everything* that goes on within their program. In the book *Legacy* by James Kerr, he shares this message: "Marginal gains: 100 things done 1 percent better to deliver cumulative competitive advantage."[1]

Taking pride in small details, even warming up, is essential in building a championship culture. The UConn Women's Basketball team proved that to me.

[1] Kerr, J. (2013). *Legacy.* London: Constable & Robinson.

COACHES' CORNER: ACTION EXERCISE

1. With your team, communicate and walk through every dynamic stretch they will be doing, ensuring every player knows how to perform each exercise correctly (see diagram).

Then, have a leader of the day or captain "echo the calls." The chosen player will yell, "High knees!" in a loud, energetic voice, and the rest of the team will respond in unison, "High knees!" The leader will then yell, "Go!" while demonstrating the footwork, distance covered, and pace to the opposite sideline.

The first attempt is not going to be as synchronized as the UConn Women's team, and that's all right. If your team follows the lead of the captain for that day, they will begin to build a foundation of a team displaying elite-level communication and unity.

I've witnessed teams that echo the calls before games. Most teams stretch quietly and will warm up with lay-up lines and shooting drills. Warming up as a united front and counting as a team sends a message to everyone in the gym that the team is locked in and ready to go!

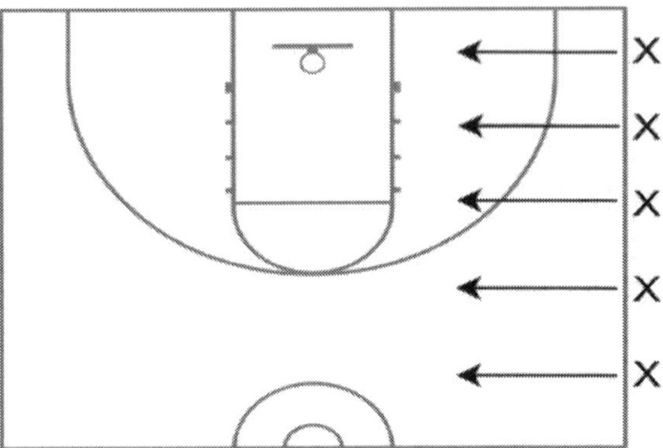

2. Another way to implement unity in stretching is by counting as a team. For example, your team can form a circle in the middle of half court and do static stretches. The team can count together from one to ten, and then end with a clap. This helps set the tone for practice, keeps everyone engaged, and prevents side

conversations. Empowering the leaders on your team to count loud and with energy will benefit everyone.

PLAYERS' PERSPECTIVE

Do you think it's important for your team to be engaged and focused during warm-ups? Why or why not?

Do you think being intentional with your warm-up will help improve communication and unity? Why or why not?

Why do you think being synchronized while warming up like the UConn Women's team would improve your team's culture?

Are you willing to take the lead in helping implement this principle? If so, ask your coach if you can discuss this principle with them.

PRINCIPLE #2
Touches

> *Act as if what you do makes a difference. It does.*
> *—William James*

A "touch" is any physical contact with a team member, such as a high five, pat on the back, or a fist bump. An interesting article titled "High Five: An MVP Move" by Julie Fournier found that "the worst teams in the NBA barely touched and had terrible body language. As a result, they consistently made selfish, inefficient plays, and their record showed it. Players who touched the most performed the best. Teams that touched the most performed the best." The article goes on to say, "Touch causes cooperation, which leads to efficient play, which determines how well a team plays. Teams that touch more, win more. High fives simply promote a greater team commitment."[2]

This past season, I attended the 2020 NCAA Division III Women's Basketball Tournament game and watched Tufts University compete against SUNY Cortland. Tufts is a great example of a team who embodies the principle of touch, as they have been a top team in the country for many years. In the past

---

[2] Fournier, Julie. "High Five: an MVP Move." *Ball Is Psych.* 4 Feb. 2019. www.basketballispsychology.com/post/high-five-an-mvp-move.

eight years, they have a combined regular-season conference record of 74–6 and have played in four final fours during that span. Creating a championship culture is time consuming, but it results in sustained success.

Ranked number two nationally in the NCAA Tournament, Tufts created a positive environment where every team member felt valued and supported each other. Every time a player subbed out of the game, each player on the bench stood up and gave their teammate a touch in the form of a high five or pat on the back. When a time-out was called, all of the bench players walked out to give their teammates high fives as they walked off the court. In the game, when a teammate was fouled or their teammate fouled a player on the opposing team, Tufts players would engage in a touch with their teammate to promote a culture of commitment to each other.

I didn't count the number of "touches" Tufts engaged in from the start of warm-ups to the end of the game, but believe me—it was a lot! If cooperation leads to more efficient playing, then I think all teams should truly embrace this principle. If the best teams do it, then so should we!

COACHES' CORNER: ACTION EXERCISE

1. During practice, establish a specific number of high fives that every player has to reach by the end of practice. Including the coaches and managers is also an option.

For example, you can pick one hundred high fives. That does not mean one player selects a teammate and gives them one hundred high fives in a row! There are many opportunities in practice when your players will have a chance to make contact with teammates.

2. Another exercise is when your team gets a water break, instruct them to simultaneously high-five as many teammates as they can. It's a rewarding thing as a coach to observe your team go out of their way to give high fives to each other. By intentionally encouraging this kind of touch, you will help your team build the habit while simultaneously giving everyone an opportunity to have fun.

PLAYERS' PERSPECTIVE

Why do think it's important to give your teammates high fives, fist bumps, and pats on the back?

Now that you learned about "touches," do you think they give teams a competitive advantage? Why or why not?

What thoughts go through your mind when your teammate makes a mistake?

How do you react when a teammate misses a wide-open lay-up or turns the ball over?

Even though you may be thinking something negative, what action(s) can you take to reflect something positive? (An example could be to give your teammate a high five and offer words of encouragement.) What is something positive you can say?

PRINCIPLE #3
Positive Talk

> *Ask yourself, "How can I make the people around me do great things?"*
> ***—Barack Obama***

In 2018, Hamilton College faced Springfield College in the Sweet Sixteen NCAA Division III Men's Basketball Tournament. Hamilton had an incredible record of 24–4 going into the game. Their team's head coach was recognized as the 2018 New England Small College Athletic Conference (NESCAC) Coach of the Year.

Thirty minutes before tip-off, I walked around the sideline and baseline where Hamilton was warming up to get to my seat. As I approached, I witnessed uplifting energy, excitement, and a plethora of high fives and positive talk.

Some examples of positive talk that successful teams participate in include:

- "Here we go, we got this!"
- "Good shot!"
- "Great pass!"
- "Don't worry about it. You got the next one."

The crowd was loud enough to make it hard for most people to even hear themselves think! Yet the players on the court seemed unbothered. They made a conscious decision to create their own energy through their actions and words.

In their warm-up, the Hamilton players were focused on helping their teammates mentally prepare for the game. They were jumping up and down, patting each other on the back, giving each other high fives, smiling at one another, and dancing when standing at the end of the line. It was clear they all had a lot of joy being on the court with their teammates.

Imagine you are on a team, and all of your teammates are focused on lifting your spirit and instilling confidence. It would be very powerful! Many teams allow the crowd or the music playing in the gym to dictate their thoughts, but Hamilton chose to communicate with each other in a way that helped them best prepare for the game.

It's essential for coaches and players to create this type of encouraging environment where everyone can have a positive influence on their team. The best part? Every team has full control over this! It's vital for *every* player to engage in positive talk, regardless if it's the team's leading scorer or a teammate who plays the least amount minutes.

Hamilton ended up losing this game in overtime. It was a hard-fought battle. After the final buzzer sounded, the players did not place blame or point fingers at one another. They displayed a high level of sportsmanship, which must have been tough to do knowing their season had ended. The Hamilton team exuded a sense of pride for being a part of something bigger than themselves, and it all started with positive talk.

COACHES' CORNER: ACTION EXERCISE

1. Educating and demonstrating to your team the importance of positive talk and body language will help these contagious behaviors become a habit. Every person has the ability to use their voice and contribute to lifting the spirits of those on the team. It is important to take time with your team to think about what phrases will help increase their confidence. Use team practices as a way to try out phrases and see what works.

When a coach embraces this principle, it will empower players to get out of their comfort zones, speak up, and use their voices to benefit the team. This will truly engage your players and also create an enjoyable and exciting environment for everyone.

PLAYERS' PERSPECTIVE

Why do you think positive talk and body language are important?

When your teammates encourage you, does it increase your confidence? Why or why not?

What phrases do you use to lift the spirits of your teammates?

If a spectator walked into the gym and watched you warm up with your team, would it be obvious that you are having fun? Why or why not?

PRINCIPLE #4

High-Five Line

> *If it's not fun, you are not doing it right.*
> *—Fran Tarkenton*

In 2019, Yale University hosted the Ivy League Men's Basketball Tournament, and I was fortunate to be able to volunteer for the event. Yale's head coach, James Jones, is a three-time Ivy League Conference Coach of the Year. With about two minutes remaining before the championship game against Harvard University, I witnessed as his players from Yale jogged over to their bench, forming a single-file line. They proceeded to engage in either a high five or creative handshake with every single teammate, then went above and beyond to include the coaches, managers, and support staff. Talk about a culture of inclusion! There was a strong *camaraderie* amongst the individuals of the Yale Men's Basketball program, and it was evident before the game even began!

Let's delve into this "high-five line" (see diagram). Once the player at the front of the line arrived at the end of the bench, he turned around to the second player in line. They then gave each other a high five, a hug, or a creative handshake they had previously made. That second player then turned around to give a handshake to the person who was behind him. This continued until every player embraced with all of their teammates.

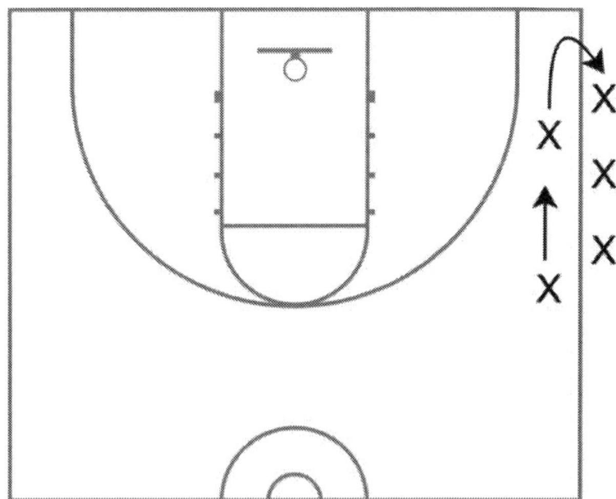

Although it sounds simple, a handshake is an opportunity for players to create their own unique embrace with a teammate. Having a handshake gives teams an extra layer of togetherness; it creates a bond between teammates and sends a message to them that their team has their back. It's incredible how impactful a quick embrace can have on someone's mindset.

That day, Yale beat Harvard and earned a spot in the NCAA Division I Tournament for only the second time in fifty-seven years. They undoubtedly had a championship culture that helped them get there.

COACHES' CORNER: ACTION EXERCISE

1. Incorporate the high-five line into your practice. For instance, directly before a twenty-minute scrimmage, your team can practice the high-five line. The teams I have watched do this usually have their players jog to the bench with about two minutes until the game starts.

The embrace between each teammate should only last a few seconds. You can recommend they practice handshakes with each other before and after practice, or any time they are together. Not every player will have a unique handshake with every teammate, and that's perfectly fine.

Even if you choose to make it simple, such as a high five or fist bump, the intention of having your team embrace one another goes a long way. It's important to reiterate that this is a fun and simple way to build team unity.

PLAYERS' PERSPECTIVE

Do you think implementing this principle will create a more inclusive and united environment? Why or why not?

Do you make sure to give a high five to every team member before the game starts? Why or why not?

Do you think participating in a creative handshake with your teammates would be fun? Why or why not?

PRINCIPLE #5
Pregame Gratitude

> *Unity is strength. Division is weakness.*
> *—Swahili proverb*

SUNY Cortland played Tufts University in the second round of the 2020 NCAA Division III Women's Basketball Tournament. Cortland, who earned SUNYAC Coaching Staff of the Year honors for the 2019–2020 season, entered this game with an impressive 22–6 record.

Before tip-off in college basketball, both teams go to their respective benches for the playing of the national anthem. The team will stand shoulder to shoulder while facing the flag, creating a straight line across the court. As the anthem plays, some players will put their hand on their heart and look at the flag, others will put their hands behind their back while closing their eyes, and some will link arms, connecting into one unit. If a team is standing single file behind one another, you can put your right hand across your heart and left arm on the shoulder of the person in front of you. The majority of the teams I observed were connected in some way, but not always. For instance, SUNY Cortland chose to grab each other's shorts. Tufts chose to put their hands over their hearts and were not connected with their teammates.

This is a principle that should be completely up to the team. It is also a great way to involve everyone in an open dialogue about what they think about before the start of the game. During the anthem, I used to think about my dad cheering me and my team on. I would think about my family, friends, and the people who have sacrificed for our country and say thank you. Lastly, I would visualize my team having fun, playing together, and giving everything we had.

It's important to play the game for reasons beyond yourself!

COACHES' CORNER: ACTION EXERCISE

1. Ask your players if they want to implement a way to stay connected during the national anthem, and if so, in what way. If your team wants to take ownership in implementing a connection, then it will add even more value to the routine. Any time a coach can empower their players to take ownership, the buy-in from the team becomes very strong. This is an example of taking pride in a small detail that has the ability to improve team culture before the game even starts!

2. There will be times when the national anthem is not played before the game. In such an instance, find a place to meet as a team, such as in a hallway or locker room. Have your team form a circle and stay connected in some way, such as with arms around each other, locking elbows, holding hands, etc. Say your final thoughts or a prayer, and break off using your team cheer.

Your team will feel more prepared to face any opponent by coming together as a team and showing support for one another before the game starts.

PLAYERS' PERSPECTIVE

Why do you think it's important to stay connected during the national anthem or during a final pregame meeting?

Do you think implementing this principle will help your team be more successful on the court? Why or why not?

Before a game begins, do you think about something or someone you are grateful for or who helps motivate you to play your best? If so, who or what do you think about?

PRINCIPLE #6

Huddle

> *Bad teams, no one leads. Average teams, coaches lead. But elite teams, players lead.*
> *—P. J. Fleck*

Hobart College played against Springfield College in the 2020 NCAA Division III Men's Basketball Tournament in the second round. Springfield College was the host school, and I felt amazed by how many fans they had as I walked into the gym and struggled to find a seat.

Hobart had defeated the University of St. Joseph team the day before. Stefan Thompson, first-year head coach of Hobart, was hired before the 2020 season. Through in-person conversations, phone calls, and text messages with Coach Thompson, I quickly learned our values aligned in regard to leadership and culture.

When playing away from your home court in an uncomfortable environment, relying on your team's culture is a must.

Hobart battled against their opponent. The Springfield student section did their part in attempting to distract the Hobart players by relentlessly cheering and screaming. I've played in games when the opposing team's fans are yelling comments like, "Scoreboard, scoreboard," and it can be hard to stay focused. Another thing out of a team's control are the referees. They always try their best to make fair calls, but it often feels like the home team gets more calls in their favor. Like any game, there will be ups and downs, and it's necessary to lean on something that is proven and concrete.

As the game progressed, I was blown away by a simple, but intentional, act Hobart consistently executed. Any time a foul was committed, whether it was for or against them, the Hobart players embraced in a tight huddle with their arms around one another. During this time, the players could engage in positive talk, empower each other, call a play, or, at the very least, come together to control their emotions.

When adversity arises, that is the most crucial time when players need to embrace in a huddle. The best teams are the ones that huddle up and actively show they have each other's back.

COACHES' CORNER: ACTION EXERCISE

1. When scrimmaging in practice, you can work on your team's huddle. Before the scrimmage begins, discuss what messages everyone thinks will most benefit the team during those few seconds huddled together. Players can say something positive, call a play, tell someone if they see a mismatch, tell a joke for comic relief, or anything else as long as they are huddling and communicating!

A coach can act as a "referee." It's important to hurry during huddles, because real referees don't want there to be long pauses in the game.

2. As their coach, you need to hold your team accountable for building this habit in practice. Most teams do not do this, and if they do, it's not on a consistent basis. *Empowering* your vocal leaders to call for the huddle, and then *praising* the players who consistently gather their teammates to huddle up will help in implementing this principle.

3. Making a hand signal that you can use from the sideline to communicate with your players to huddle up is another great tool.

Any opportunity a team can use to come together, show mutual support for one another, communicate a message, and stay united should be taken advantage of!

PLAYERS' PERSPECTIVE

How do you think implementing the huddle will help your team, especially if playing in a loud environment with a lot of cheering and screaming?

How does your team act under pressure when the other team is playing well, and your team is struggling?

Do you stay fully engaged in the game, regardless of if you are playing or on the bench, or do you let the crowd affect you?

During both practices and games, what actions and words do you communicate to your team when adversity arises?

Do you take ownership in making sure your teammates huddle together to communicate positive talk, empower each other, or call a play? If so, is it a tight huddle (arms around each other with all players making eye contact)?

PRINCIPLE #7
Point to the Passer

> *It is amazing what you can accomplish if you do not care who gets the credit.*
> *—Harry S. Truman*

Dean Smith, former head coach for the University of North Carolina (UNC) Men's Basketball team (1961–1997), led his team to two national championships in 1982 and 1993. UNC has won six national championships, with their most recent one coming in 2017. He emphasized pointing to the passer after every made basket.

If you watch any basketball game, from youth to professional, you will likely see a player make a three-pointer or a lay-up as the result of a great pass. In most cases, the player who scored the basket usually uses the few seconds after to celebrate in some way. The culture of celebrating your own success after a made basket has become the norm in today's game. It also reveals a "me, me, me" mindset, not a team-first mentality.

If you watch a UNC Men's game, you will notice players driving hard to the basket and selflessly zipping the ball to one another. When a player does make a basket for UNC, the player who scored will often point to their teammate who helped create the scoring opportunity.

A "hockey assist" is when someone makes a pass to a teammate, and that teammate makes a pass to another teammate, resulting in a made basket. Some teams keep track of hockey assists to include even more players in the made basket. In order to motivate your team, players and coaches must praise selfless acts, like pointing to a teammate after an assist.

Ultimately, the great teams find ways to share the credit in a sport that truly values putting the team first.

COACHES' CORNER: ACTION EXERCISE

1. In practice, your team can participate in a shooting drill with emphasis placed on pointing to the passer (see diagram). For example, you can have a line on the top of the key (with basketballs) and a line on the right wing. The first player with the ball in their hands dribbles full speed by a coach or imaginary defender, then must get two feet into the paint before passing. The player on the wing will sprint to the corner and call out to the player with the ball to communicate to their teammate where they are on the court. If the shot goes in, the player that scored can point to their teammate and add in a phrase like, "Great pass, Sarah," or "Good look, Mike," to acknowledge their teammate and give them credit. The passer can get the rebound and then switch lines. Similarly, on a miss, a teammate who misses a shot can still acknowledge the great pass and praise their teammate for getting them an open shot.

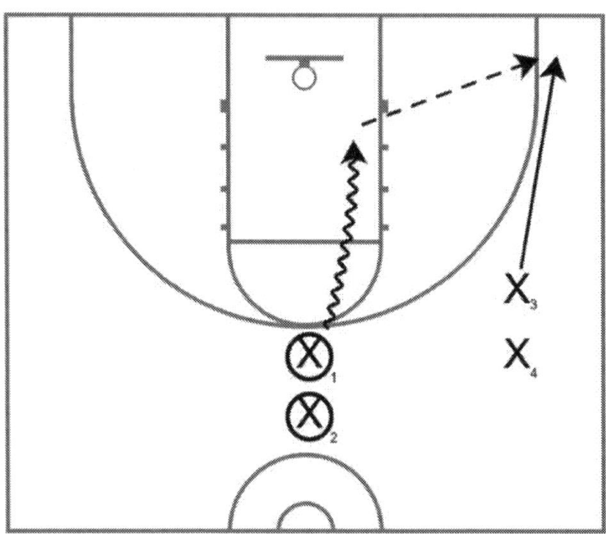

PLAYERS' PERSPECTIVE

What message does it send to your teammates when they give you a great pass, and you verbally acknowledge and point to them?

Do you think it's important to celebrate your teammates' on-court successes? If yes, please provide an example of how you show your teammates you're happy for them when they do well.

Why do you think sharing the credit of made baskets will help build a more cohesive team culture?

Do you think there is a correlation between sharing the credit and winning? Why or why not?

Do you practice pointing to the passer when playing pickup with your teammates in the off season? Why or why not?

PRINCIPLE #8

Help Them Up

> *There is no exercise better for the heart than reaching down and lifting people up.*
> *—John Holmes*

In 2018, Villanova played Kansas in the NCAA Division I Men's Basketball semifinal game. Both of these programs have elite basketball teams. Villanova University has won three national championships, with the 2018 championship being the most recent. The University of Kansas has won three national championships, as well.

I was home with my two brothers watching this much-anticipated showdown. Villanova, led by head coach Jay Wright, had a seventeen-point lead in the second half with 7:08 on the clock. At this point, one of Villanova's players, Jalen Brunson, stole the ball. He was immediately fouled and fell hard to the ground. Within three seconds, all four of his teammates on the court had sprinted over to help him up. In that moment, his team showed they truly had each other's backs and cared for one another.

In games, players should always get up off the ground as fast as they can and make an effort to get back into the play. However, if a whistle is blown to stop the play, all four on-court teammates should be there within seconds to help their fallen teammate up.

Unfortunately, it is common to see situations where a player will get fouled to the ground and maybe one teammate will run over to help him or her up. When a player falls on the ground and then helps him or herself up alone, it sends a message that the team lacks unity and commitment to one another. It needs to become second nature for players to help their teammates off the ground whenever there is a stoppage in the game.

Over the years I have admired the championship culture that Coach Wright has built within his program. Villanova is a perfect example of a team that values helping a teammate up, because they understand the importance of what it truly means to be a great teammate.

An exceptional quote for any team to keep in mind was said by NBA Hall of Fame Coach Phil Jackson: "The strength of the team is each individual. The strength of each member is the team." As a player, knowing every one of your teammates has your back creates a culture that will inspire the group to give everything they have for one another.

COACHES' CORNER: ACTION EXERCISE

1. Your players can get repetitions helping their teammates up and building this habit in scrimmage situations. Additionally, directly after helping up a teammate is a perfect time to get into that quick huddle discussed in Principle #6.

2. Another fun drill is to have one player stand near half court while facing their teammates, who are spread out (see diagram). Have players separated by at least five feet from each other by using the whole half court. The player at half court is the leader of the drill, and everyone else attempts to copy their every move. The leader starts by doing foot-fires for a few seconds. They can then slide to the left, slide to the right, and jump up for a rebound for about fifteen to thirty seconds. The player leading the group (or the coach) can yell, "Charge!" Then the player at half court safely falls backward, simulating a charge, while *all* teammates sprint over to *help them up*. Only two teammates can grab each hand to help them up, but the rest of the team should give them a pat on the back or a high five after the leader is back on their feet. This is a very fun way to incorporate this principle, and the players I have done this with always seem to enjoy it.

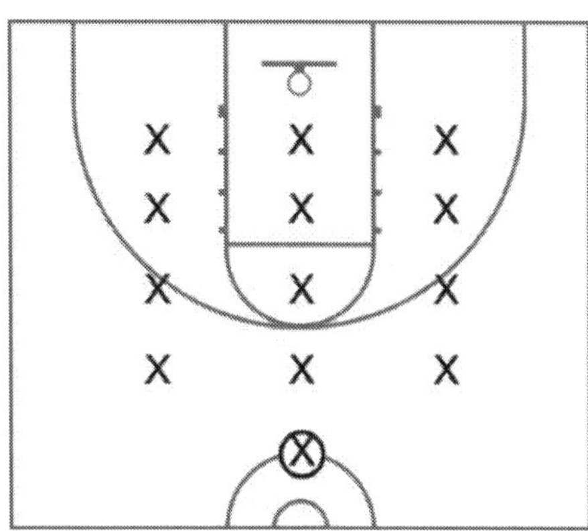

PLAYERS' PERSPECTIVE

Why do you think it's important to help your teammates up off the ground?

Do you show your teammates that you have their backs by consistently executing this principle? Why or why not?

Do all four of your teammates sprint over to help you up off the ground? If not, do you think it's important to communicate to them why this is important?

If an opposing player falls to the ground next to you, do you help him or her up to demonstrate true sportsmanship? Why or why not?

PRINCIPLE #9

Touch 5

> *If it is important to you, you will find a way. If not, you'll find an excuse.*
> *—Ryan Blair*

A "touch 5" is when all five teammates on the court touch after the first free throw. As mentioned in Principle #2, this can consist of a high five or pat on the back. The two players standing on the lane line can give high fives, and the players outside of the arc can give a pat on the back or high five. No matter what, all four players can offer encouraging words. The emphasis is that all five players on the court make an effort to connect with each other after the first free throw.

In 2019–2020, the University of Virginia Men's Basketball team hosted Duke University in an Atlantic Coast Conference regular-season game. Virginia was led by Tony Bennett, who is well known for creating a strong team culture on the court. The score was 51–50 with Virginia leading when Duke intentionally fouled a player on Virginia. Virginia was in the double bonus, meaning they were headed to the free-throw line to shoot two free throws with 3.7 seconds left in the game.

Tony Bennett elected to have none of his players positioned on the lane line when his player was shooting. Coaches will use this tactic so their team doesn't have to sprint back on defense after the shot. It also prevents potential violations or fouls from occurring during the free throw.

The Virginia player shot the first free throw and missed. We can only imagine all the thoughts going through the five Virginia players' heads who were in the game at that moment. *Do we have a foul to give? What defense are we in? Who am I guarding?* However, despite the in-game pressures, two Virginia players sprinted over to give their teammate a pat on the back. Those two players demonstrated the belief they had in their teammate to make the next shot. In this particular situation, the two other teammates were on the opposite end of the court closely guarding their assigned players. The Virginia player went on to make the second free throw to go up by two and beat the number-seven-ranked team in the country at the time.

It's important that players understand the importance of encouraging their teammates and take accountability over this principle.

COACHES' CORNER: ACTION EXERCISE

1. You can practice a "touch 5" in a team scrimmage (see diagram). Coaches can officiate, and any time there is a shooting foul, all four players should participate in a "touch 5." This happens after the first free throw if a player is shooting two shots. The free-throw shooter usually takes one step forward to give a high five to their teammates positioned on the lane line as they simultaneously step toward the shooter. The two players outside the arc step inside to give their teammate a high five or pat on the back.

2. Another way to practice this is to split your team into groups of three or five to shoot free throws at different baskets. For a group of three, the two players will align themselves in the correct position inside the arc on the lane line, as if they were in a game. After the shot, regardless of a make or miss, both will step toward their teammate who is shooting and give them a high five. They should also add words of encouragement like, "You got this, Julia," "I know you're going to make the next shot, Prince," or "Stay confident, Liz. I believe in you."

In high school, my teammate Sam would run over and instill confidence in me by saying, "You got this," and by patting me on the back. In college, my teammate DaRay would encourage me with a high five and by saying, "Fingertips," because that helped me focus on my shooting mechanics.

Feeling that belief and support from your four teammates, as well as your teammates and coaches on the bench, helps eliminate self-doubt.

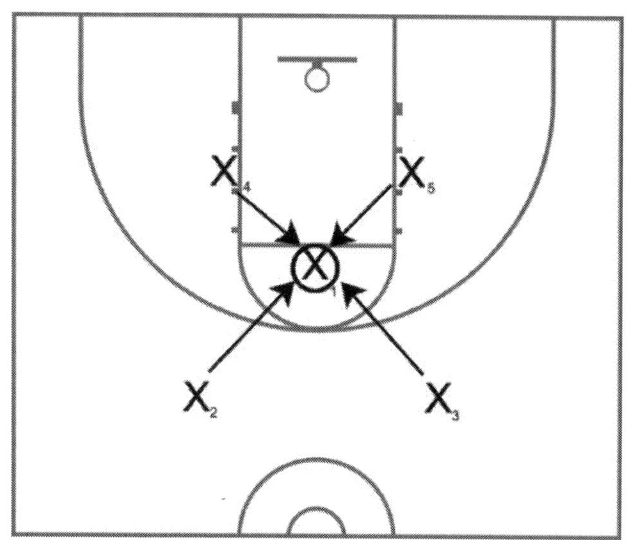
X_4
X_5
X_1
X_2
X_3

PLAYERS' PERSPECTIVE

Why do you think it's important to show your teammates you believe in them through your actions and words when they are on the free-throw line?

Do you make a conscious effort to make contact with your teammates and offer encouraging words? Why or why not?

Have you been on the free-throw line late in a game when the score was close with a lot of pressure on you? If so, how did it feel?

Do you think it would help if your teammates and coach encouraged you? If the answer is yes, be that person for your teammates!

PRINCIPLE #10
Time-Outs

> *We are what we repeatedly do. Excellence, then, is not an act, but a habit.*
> ***—Will Durant***

> *A single arrow is easily broken, but not ten in a bundle.*
> ***—Japanese proverb***

Swarthmore College, ranked number six in the country, faced number-five-ranked Randolph-Macon College in the 2019 NCAA Division III Men's Basketball Tournament in the Sweet 16. I had watched Swarthmore in person the previous year, and what stood out to me the most was their togetherness and team-first mentality. At this game, I was able to watch in person what a championship culture looked like!

During the duration of a basketball game, both teams are allotted a specific number of time-outs. However, what each team does with those precious seconds varies drastically. It was evident that Swarthmore had rehearsed exactly what the most effective and efficient setup was for their team.

First, they quickly jogged off the court into the time-out to save time, as opposed to slowly walking over to the sideline.

Walking over to the sideline is an inefficient way to utilize the limited seconds your team has to communicate with each other. During Swarthmore's full time-out, the five players in the game sat on the bench and the assistant coaches stood behind it. By standing behind, the assistant coaches could hear and see what the head coach was communicating and drawing on the whiteboard. They also blocked the vision of fans in the crowd. The rest of the team circled around the players sitting on the bench. Every single member of the team was fully engaged in what their head coach was saying. He was able to make eye contact with anyone on the team with a quick head movement.

Great leaders make eye contact with the people with whom they are speaking, and their audience reciprocates by showing they are actively listening with their eyes, words, and body language. The players on the bench were extremely focused on their head coach's instructions during time-outs.

The players made sure to stay connected in some way. They either had their arms around each other or held each other's shorts. While it looked odd and different from anything I had seen before, that was how they chose to stay connected during time-outs. After all, small intentional acts that make you 1 percent better all add up.

It takes extra energy for a team to quickly jog off the court, get in a formation, stay engaged, and connect with teammates, but it pays off in the long run. It's evident why Swarthmore was one of the most connected groups in college basketball and were the number-one ranked Division III team in the country in 2020.

COACHES' CORNER: ACTION EXERCISE

1. Discuss with your team why you don't want any of them looking into the crowd or having side conversations during time-outs. Instead, collectively determine which formation during the time-out works best for you and your team, and walk through it so everyone is on the same page.

Additionally, if you coach a team where there is a water cooler at your bench, make sure to communicate that you expect there to be water ready to be passed out during time-outs in games. Players need to hydrate during this short rest period, and this saves valuable seconds!

2. In practice, you can yell "time-out" and simulate going through a late-game situation with a thirty or sixty-second time-out. Pick five players to be in the game, then see if the formation is what you want and if your team can execute the play you draw up with no defense guarding them. During this time, it's critical to have everyone listening to the game plan when a coach is speaking. This principle is important to maximizing your limited time with your players, and it needs to be prioritized. This is something that may require a little more time to develop, but is definitely worth the investment. It helps prepare everyone when it's their time to be sitting in one of those five seats on the bench during a game.

It's also important for coaches to be knowledgeable on what they are saying to their team. A common theme I've noticed is the lack of in-game adjustments made from the original game plan. The coaching staff needs to be able to adjust the game plan if it's not working. If players respect you and your knowledge of the game, your team's execution on the court will be tough to stop on both ends of the floor!

3. Empowering your players to call time-outs on their own in situations they feel are necessary is another great way to emphasize the team-first mentality. Players need to have a high basketball IQ to execute this. It's common to play in a very loud gym where it's hard to hear the coach from the other side of the court. Teaching players through practice, games, and film study can lead to your team gaining an extra possession to potentially win a game. Simulating a loud, rowdy gym by having your team cheer loudly or by using a stereo system to play music is a great way to practice high-pressure situations. Creating an environment where your players have to make quick decisions will also help translate to a more confident team during games.

PLAYERS' PERSPECTIVE

Why do you think it's important to be efficient with the allotted time when a time-out is called?

Do you quickly jog off the court when a time-out is called, or do you slowly walk off and take your time? Which one helps build a championship culture, and why?

Do you stay connected with your teammates by putting your arms around them?

In past time-outs, did you make eye contact with your head coach to communicate with your eyes and body language that you were paying attention?

In past time-outs, when you weren't currently in the game, were you in a position where you could see and hear what your coach was explaining to the team?

Do you think it's important to make sure water is ready for your teammates when you are on the bench? Why or why not?

PRINCIPLE #11

Next-Play

> *Don't give up. Don't ever give up.*
> *—Jim Valvano*

> *Tough times never last, but tough people do.*
> *—Robert H. Schuller*

In the 2018 NCAA Division I Men's Basketball Tournament, Texas Tech, Purdue, West Virginia, and Villanova all gathered in Boston, Massachusetts, at the TD Garden for the Sweet 16 and Elite Eight rounds of March Madness. I was a volunteer at the event and allowed behind-the-scenes access for a few days. It was amazing to observe the elite-level teams interact with one another. This is the stage players have dreamed about playing on since they were kids! At that point in the season, every team was focused on making a run to the final four and winning a national championship.

Texas Tech's head coach, Chris Beard, is a great leader, and I have followed his team ever since that weekend in 2018. They are relentless and compete with a "next-play" mentality. "Next-play" means to control what you can and not dwell on a play that already happened. Whether you make a lay-up, miss a shot, get scored on, or get a steal, you move on to the next play.

Texas Tech has been one of the best defensive teams in the country, and they have executed this principle consistently since hiring Coach Beard in 2016. They sprint back in transition, communicate with teammates, and do everything in their power to get a stop on the defensive end.

A lot of basketball players don't make an effort to sprint back when their team is losing by a lot, when they are too tired, or when they don't get a foul call. This is when the "me, me, me" mindset—instead of the team-first mentality—takes over a player's decision-making. I bet a lot of people reading this can think of a time they, a teammate, or an opponent didn't run back on defense for a plethora of reasons!

Texas Tech has proven that being in "next-play" mode contributes to a championship culture. They also don't point fingers. If a player turns the ball over, instead of yelling at each other and reacting, they give each other a high five and move on to the next play. It's important to give encouragement, belief, and support to teammates, even on a nonpositive play. This is a common theme for great teams.

One of the most selfish things a player can do in the game of basketball is *choose* not to sprint back on defense. When this happens, that player is sending a clear message to their coaches and teammates that they just don't care enough about the team's success. I have seen players not summon the energy to run back on defense, so they "cherry-pick." This means when a player's team loses possession of the ball on offense, that player chooses to stay on the other end of the court next to the basket they are trying to score on without making an effort to run back in transition. When their team gets the ball, one of their teammates will throw it to the opposite end of the court, resulting in a wide-open lay-up for the player who did not play any defense. Most people who have played basketball can relate to this—and may be guilty of it, as well!

Making the "next-play" mentality a habit and expected behavior will vastly improve a team's ability to limit the other team from scoring opportunities. Embracing unavoidable challenges that occur throughout a basketball game will lead to a team that is collectively resilient and confident in every situation.

COACHES' CORNER: ACTION EXERCISE

1. Having the "next-play" mentality will help build a culture of *controlling what you can control.* During practice, put your team through drills that challenge them. For example, practice a full-court lay-up drill where the team has to make a specific number of lay-ups in a minute. (see diagram) Make the target number challenging—maybe one that is unrealistic for the allotted time. See which players give 100 percent effort until the time runs out, regardless of how impossible it may seem, and which players give up. Creating this mindset of giving your best effort and never taking a play-off is a difficult habit to build. However, if you choose to structure your practice in a way where players get a lot of repetitions with a "next-play" mentality, it will enhance your championship culture.

2. Another exercise is to have your team scrimmage one another. Have one team start with a specific number of points, and put the other team at a disadvantage with a specific number of points. For example, one team starts with ten points and the other team starts with zero. The game can be played to fifteen or twenty-one. Watch each player closely, and see if the team that is losing gives up or if they take it one play at a time, compete, and fight their way back into the game.

Mental toughness can be described as the ability to face adversity and continue to persevere without giving up. It will become very clear to you as the coach which players possess this important mindset. It's a given that there will be obstacles faced in every basketball game. Preparing your team in practice to embrace adversity head on, knowing the team has their back, will help build the habit of playing through mistakes.

In basketball, coaches can often micromanage and correct players' mistakes immediately. If you can take a step back, watch your team compete during this segment, and take some handwritten or mental notes, it can add a lot of value to your team. Discussing with your team their thoughts on individual and team performance, and then sharing yours, will create a powerful dialogue that will lead to collective improvement.

These two exercises are great ways to have conversations with your team about the "next-play" mentality. The purpose is to evaluate which players give their all, no matter what the scoreboard says, and which players need to improve their "next-play" mentality. On days when your offense isn't scoring, relying on your team's defense is a must! If every player who steps on the court is on a mission to prevent the other team from scoring, your team will have a chance to be competitive in most games.

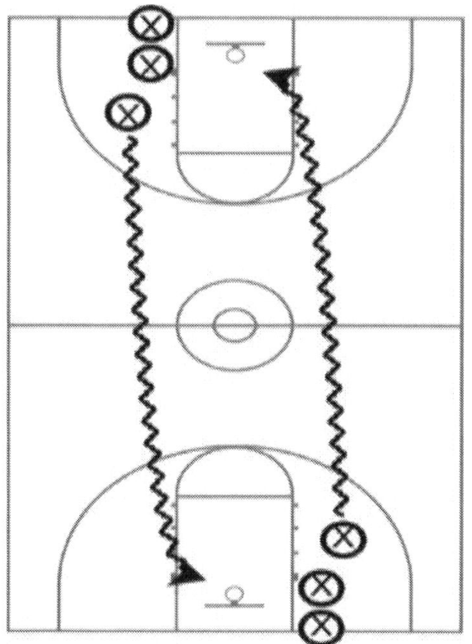

PLAYERS' PERSPECTIVE

Why do you think it's important to play with the "next-play" mentality?

Do you consistently sprint back as fast you can on defense, communicate with your teammates, and finish the play by boxing out the player you were guarding? Why or why not?

Can your teammates and coaches count on you to always have a "next-play" mentality, or just when things are going well for you and your team?

When your teammate turns the ball over or misses a lay-up, do you encourage them to focus on the "next-play", or do you get upset with them? Moving forward, what phrase(s) can you say to help them stay positive?

PRINCIPLE #12
Bench

> *The important thing is that your teammates have to know you're pulling for them and you really want them to be successful.*
> *—Kobe Bryant*

> *You don't inspire your teammates by showing them how amazing you are. You inspire them by showing them how amazing they are.*
> *—Robyn Benincasa*

Now, a lot of people know about the Monmouth University Men's Basketball bench celebrations of 2015. They "rowed the boat," shot invisible bows and arrows, etc., which took the nation by storm when highlighted on ESPN. While it's true every team is different in their approach, the best teams have fun on the bench while being serious and supportive of their teammates on the court.

In 2020, Conard High School boys' varsity basketball played Plainfield High School in the Connecticut Interscholastic Athletic Conference state tournament game. I drove over to Conard High, located in West Hartford, to cheer on a former teammate of mine, Mark Corey, who was serving as the head junior varsity and assistant varsity coach. Conard had secured a home game for the first time since 1996, and there was a lot of excitement in the gym.

Throughout the game, Conard's bench support was absolutely amazing! Every single player on the team had great body language and cheered on their teammates. Every time Conard scored or got a stop, the bench yelled, jumped up and down, and truly gave all of their energy to their teammates on the court. Not only was the bench going wild, but the Conard student section was modeling the same energy through chants and clapping! The gym environment was loud, supportive, and contagious. Conard ended up winning by thirty-one points, and it was the best team win I had ever seen from a high-school basketball team.

I asked Mark a few days later how they got everyone to buy in. He said, "We praise the guys on the bench in film sessions and let them know they add a ton of value." A lot of those bench players ended up playing in that game, and the starters were just as excited for them when they were in the spotlight and contributing on the court.

A bench has the ability to lift the morale of the players on the court. Players engaged on the bench show they are contributing to the championship-culture environment despite not being in the game at that current moment. It's a special thing when the starters cheer on the bench players and vice versa, and the Conard Boys' Basketball team is a perfect example of this principle.

COACHES' CORNER: ACTION EXERCISE

1. Explain to your players the importance of cheering on the team. Players who sit on the bench during a game, need to know that their positive energy on the bench, adds value to the team. They all need to understand that their contribution every day in practice is just as important as the players who play on game day, because they helped prepare them.

2. In practice and throughout drills, players should be saying the *names* of their teammates and yelling out encouraging words. Elite-level programs, like the UConn Women's Basketball team, have created a culture of consistently saying each other's names. This forces players to create their own energy while not relying on music or anything else to get them pumped up. The concept of using words to energize team members directly translates to the bench during games when your team needs to maintain or increase energy. The maturity levels of your players play into this, but a rule that can be implemented is "Only *cheer* for your teammates. There is no yelling at the referees, the opposing team's players, or fans." There are so many words a team can use to cheer on their own team without saying anything demeaning to the referees, the opposing team's players, or fans.

3. Using film is a great tool to evaluate the performance of your team's bench during games. You can ask someone to film the game from an angle where you can see the bench's reaction, then discuss positive and negative body language during team sessions. Creating an environment where feedback is accepted rather than feared will lead to a successful and sustained culture. Players want to improve and be coached, and this is a great way to hold everyone accountable.

4. Lastly, presenting a "Best Teammate Award" at the end of the season can serve as another way to motivate your team. The

award should be given to a player who always supports his or her teammates during practice, in games, and from the bench, regardless of whether or not they play frequently.

PLAYERS' PERSPECTIVE

Do you think your support and encouragement from the bench contributes to positive team morale and a championship culture? Why or why not?

If there was a camera filming your personal bench reactions during games, what behaviors would a spectator see from you?

What words or phrases do you use from the bench to encourage your teammates throughout the game?

Does your team consistently cheer each other on from the bench? If yes, provide a few examples.

PRINCIPLE #13
Communication

> *We communicate all the time, even when we don't realize it. Be aware of body language.*
> *—Pat Summitt*

> *Communication does not always occur naturally, even among a tight-knit group of individuals. Communication must be taught and practiced in order to bring everyone together as one.*
> *—Mike Krzyzewski*

Tufts University Women's Basketball was the number-two-ranked team in the nation going into the 2020 NCAA Tournament. They made it to the Sweet 16 before their season was cut short due to the COVID-19 pandemic. They are a perfect example of building a culture where everyone feels valued, contributes, and has fun playing the game of basketball. Having watched them in person versus SUNY Cortland and in many games online during the season, it's evident their head coach, Jill Pace, did an amazing job in her first season with the team in 2019–2020.

Player-to-player communication is vital in building a championship culture. The Tufts players seemed to communicate with each other in a very respectful way. On top of constant encouragement from all members of the team through actions and words, they also handled turnovers and mistakes in the game positively. They didn't point fingers after a missed shot, a traveling violation, or throwing the ball out of bounds. Instead, they moved on to the next play and even gave each other high fives after a mistake. Tufts definitely has the right players in their program, which is why they communicate with each other at an elite level.

Coach-to-player communication has a direct correlation on a team's performance, too. *While each player should be treated equally, not every player should be coached the same.* Everyone accepts feedback in different ways, and learning the best communication styles for every member of the team is necessary as a coach.

After a phone conversation with Coach Pace, it's evident to me that she emphasizes open communication with her players. She communicates with her players about anything they want to talk about, whether it's about basketball, academics, or life. This allows her to build relationships based on trust and learn more about each individual, and for them to learn more about their coach in return. By creating a connection with everyone on the team, Coach Pace shows she cares about each *person* in her program, not just the player.

Coach-to-referee communication style is another extremely important facet to a team's on-court success. Watching Tufts play this season, I noticed how Coach Pace always remained poised on the sideline, and I truly admire the way she interacted with referees. Even if a referee incorrectly made a call or missed something on the court, she always showed respect. Too often, I see coaches using the sideline as an opportunity to yell at, demean, or even make fun of the officials. Would that behavior be acceptable if the coach were in a grocery store, bank, or park? Why do coaches *choose* to behave this way?

Players are always watching their coach, and if the coach isn't being respectful to the referee, why should the players? If a team observes this behavior, it will lead to players complaining to referees, which does not resemble a championship culture. The job of a head coach is to prepare their team to battle through adversity on the court and lead by example when communicating to officials. As the leader, coaches have the responsibility to remain calm as much as possible.

What message does it send to a team when the head coach's emotions get the best of him or her, and he or she gets a technical foul? I fully support a coach standing up for players, but it needs to be done in a respectful way.

COACHES' CORNER: ACTION EXERCISE

1. Provide your players some time to self-reflect. Have them write down the way in which they prefer to be coached and why. The "why" is super important, because most players may have never thought about this before.

For example, a player may write, "I feel I play best when my coach doesn't yell at me directly after a mistake. I am already so hard on myself, and when I make a mistake and the coach yells at me, it makes it hard for me to move on to the next play. I'd prefer to play through my mistakes during the game and have a one-on-one conversation with my coach afterward." Those who have played sports can relate to being yelled at after messing up. In those moments, it's usually best not to yell at your players. However, if a player is motivated by yelling, and that has been communicated through one-on-one conversations, then adjusting your coaching style accordingly is necessary for that player. If the mistake was very significant, then subbing out the player and having the head coach, assistant coach, or even a player talk with them is a great way to communicate the information to them. When you have time and if you think it will serve as a teachable moment, discuss with your players individually why they were taken out of the game in specific situations. Players want to play, and if they can find ways to stay on the court, they usually will take the feedback in a positive way.

It may be asking a lot of coaches to personalize their coaching style for every player; however, having that information can make a huge difference in getting the best effort out of each individual!

2. Players can repeat this exercise in regard to their preferred communication style with their teammates. Having such open dialogue can improve performance because players will know how to best communicate with specific teammates. These types

of conversations will feel more natural if done in the context of a team meeting or through some of the team-building exercises outlined at the end of this book.

3. Coaches in the middle or high-school levels who have limited time with their teams can make themselves available for a specific amount of time before or after practice. I have heard of coaches who make themselves accessible for thirty minutes before or after every practice. During this time, any player can meet with the coach to talk about basketball, academics, or anything else going on in their life. Asking the players open-ended questions and allowing them to steer the conversation is important. An example of a powerful question: "What is one thing I should know about you that will help me coach you better?" This is a great way to build a strong foundation of open communication both on and off the court.

4. Lastly, as the head coach, learning the names of the officials before the game and shaking their hands is crucial. Setting this example for your team and doing everything in your power to help them succeed says a lot about you as a leader. Instead of yelling, "Ref!" when you want their attention, you can use the referee's first name. Dale Carnegie said, "Remember that a person's name is to that person the sweetest and most important sound in any language." Throughout the season, it's likely you will have the same referees working your games. Building a rapport with them, as well as a reputation of treating them with respect while also standing up for your team, will play into your favor . . . especially if the opposing coach is not communicating with the referees politely!

PLAYERS' PERSPECTIVE

How do you communicate with your teammates in games when they play well? How about when they play poorly? Is it the same? Why or why not?

Are you respectful when communicating with the referees? Why or why not?

Do you feel comfortable talking with your coach or teammates if you need help with something, basketball-related or not? Why or why not?

What actions can you take to improve communication with your teammates? (Examples: Go early or stay late after practice to hang out and talk with your team, ask open-ended questions, practice extra drills together, etc.)

Write down the way you prefer to be coached, both in practice and games, that you feel leads to you performing to your full potential, and why. (Example: play through mistakes and discuss with your coach after the practice or game, how you can improve.)

PRINCIPLE #14
Accountability Circle

> *What divides us pales in comparison to what unites us.*
> *—Edward Kennedy*

Coach Joe Mantegna is the head coach of the varsity boys' basketball team at Blair Academy in New Jersey. He has coached players who have gone on to play in the NBA and numerous high-level college basketball programs.

I was fortunate to volunteer at two USA youth development basketball clinics where he spoke about team culture. Coach Mantegna shared an exercise he uses with his team called, "the circle of accountability." With my teams, I call it the, "accountability circle." I have used the accountability circle at the end of practice and it definitely helped enhance our team's culture.

Our team would meet at half court and position themselves in a circle so everyone could make eye contact with each other. Each person in the circle put their arms around each other, but a team can choose to stay connected any way that feels comfortable. The purpose of this meeting is to hold each other accountable. The head coach makes it clear from day one and then continuously reiterates that what is said in the circle, stays in the circle. Initially, the only comments that are made will be words of praise and positive reinforcement. It's a time to compliment individual players for their actions that helped the team improve that day.

It's also important to mention that the coaches should not be the first to speak, if possible. There may be some awkward silences, but a player can be a leader and speak up to start the conversation.

The activity begins with any player in the circle praising a team member. For example, Bilal can share, "I want to give a shoutout to Jeff. If you look at him, his shirt is drenched in sweat and he is still out of breath. He gave his best effort in every single drill today and motivated me to work harder, even when I felt like I had no more energy left. In our scrimmage, he boxed his player out every time and dove on the ground for a loose ball. If we all give the same type of effort like Jeff gave today, I know we can reach our full potential as a team."

Doing this activity at the end of practice provides a platform for immediate feedback. It allows everyone to have a voice and encourages positive behaviors. Regardless if you're a starter or a bench player, your actions can and should be praised if they are helping the team improve.

When a team becomes comfortable with this exercise, the advanced level of holding each other accountable for poor behaviors can be implemented. It's important to be patient, because this principle can only be executed in a safe space, so a team needs to ease into it or else it can turn into a reserved and defensive environment.

An example of a respectful dialogue would be Bonni sharing, "Rita, you are definitely one of our best players and a leader on this team. However, you didn't consistently run back on defense, which resulted in the other team scoring a few easy transition lay-ups. You also didn't call out a back screen, and our team got scored on because of your lack of communication. You have proven to all of us you are capable of doing these things, but we need you to do it every single play."

This is an honest and effective way for anyone to voice their opinion on how some behaviors hinder the team's performance. This example highlights strictly addressing the *behavior* of a teammate on the basketball court—nothing personal.

If what was said was inappropriate or not helpful in regard to the team's success, the head coach can explain, "I hear what you're saying, but I disagree" and then explain their reasoning.

Implementing this at the last ten minutes of every practice will improve trust, communication, unity, and build a culture of accountability.

COACHES' CORNER: ACTION EXERCISE

1. Immediately implement this principle at the end of every practice! If your team fully commits to using this safe space, the team can take that next step to improving on the court. Over time, the conversations will improve, but it has to be done every day.

As mentioned in the beginning of the book, our time is limited; 120 minutes in a two-hour practice is not a lot. However, this principle is worth the investment. Not only does it create a space for your team to grow as individuals and as a team every single day, it teaches players how to communicate with people outside of the basketball court effectively and respectfully. Coaches often want to implement exercises like this, but get caught up in adding a ton of plays during their limited time. At minimum, ten minutes should be used to enhance team culture using the accountability circle at the end of every practice.

2. This principle can and should be used after every game, as well. Emotions are high after a game, but allowing the players who battled on the floor to express their feelings can help the coaching staff better understand what went right or wrong from a player's perspective. As the coach, you have so many different things going on in your mind during practices and games. Players have a lot on their mind, as well, but they are the ones on the court playing. Don't you think their insight can add a ton of value?

After a while, players learn what a coach truly cares about in regard to on-the-court performance and team culture. Allowing them to share—and most likely confirm what you were going to say—means a lot more to their teammates. This time is not to be used to point fingers or place blame, but rather as a time when players can speak up and use their voice to help the team improve.

It's rare for coaches to have this type of open communication, but it allows an open dialogue that can provide valuable information.

3. In some instances, I have had the whole team go around the circle and say what they need to do better for the team to be successful. One by one, they spoke up and I wrote down what they said. For example, Matt might say, "I need to box out better. I need to find a body, drive them back, and make sure we secure the rebound before running down the court." Then, Matt cannot use "boxing out" as something he needs to do better in any future games. Everyone on the team knows what Matt wants to get better at, so everyone can hold him accountable and assist him in improving.

When a player is vulnerable and acknowledges where they failed their teammates, most of them will have a sense of pride and take accountability for their actions in the following games. This behavior should be vocally praised by the coaching staff, because players are holding themselves accountable in a vulnerable way in front of the entire team. This is a great way to build your team and see progress throughout the course of a season.

PLAYERS' PERSPECTIVE

How do you think this open and honest dialogue will help improve your team's performance on the court?

Why do you think it's important to find opportunities to speak up and praise your teammates?

Do you think it's important (to both yourself and your team) to hold yourself accountable by evaluating your own performance after every practice and game? Why or why not?

Provide an example of a time you held a teammate accountable by sharing feedback in a respectful way.

WE OVER ME

> *Ask not what your teammates can do for you. Ask what you can do for your teammates.*
> *—Magic Johnson*

My twin brother, Ben, worked as an undergraduate manager and then as a graduate assistant coach for the men's basketball team at Syracuse University. Working as a manager for an elite program is very similar to being a great teammate. As a manager, you take advantage of every opportunity to add value to the team. Some managerial duties in practice consist of rebounding, passing, using a football pad to simulate contact, cleaning up sweat after a player falls over, charting statistics, giving high fives, and clapping. You have to be 100 percent committed, have a positive attitude, and be willing to do a variety of tasks to help the team with little to no recognition.

When you're on the team, even if you're the last roster spot, there's a possibility you will play. As a manager, you show up every day because you love the game of basketball. In 2014, I watched Ben clean up sweat on ESPN as an undergraduate manager and thought that was the coolest thing. Five years later, in 2019, Syracuse beat the number-one-ranked Duke University at Cameron Indoor Stadium while Ben was working as the graduate assistant coach. I was just as proud when he shook Zion Williamson's hand on national television after the game ...

well, maybe a little bit more excited! Ben was a great teammate and was recognized for his commitment to the team over his six years, but he never did it for the praise.

At Syracuse, a lot of undergraduate students want to be involved with the program, but only the ones who pass the interview are offered positions. The interview process consists of meeting with head managers (juniors and seniors), who ask you a variety of questions. Ben shared that the most important question he was asked was, "Why do you want to be a manager?" A very common question, but one that holds a lot of weight. The interviewees are looking for answers that show the person is committed to helping the team be successful in any way they can. Being a manager is a perfect example of people who have a passion for the game of basketball, have a team-first mentality, and who love being part of a team!

In 2019–2020, the chemistry of the players on the team resulted in some big wins. If you watched a Syracuse game during that year and looked over to the bench, you would see a group of individuals committed to something bigger than themselves. Managers sitting behind the bench at home games were standing up, celebrating, and smiling! There is a saying: "Body language screams." Well, I didn't see any bad body language on their bench. Rather, I saw a unified team that cared about their teammates. Everyone in the program had the same mentality: When the players in the game succeed, we all succeed.

A very kind gesture the Syracuse Men's Basketball program does is present graduating managers with a gift toward the end of the season. In front of a banquet audience of roughly a few hundred people, each manager is given an opportunity to speak about what their time as a member of the program has meant to them. Each senior is allowed to invite family members to this very special event. Lastly, each graduating manager receives a framed, orange-colored "S"—something they can keep with them to symbolize their time spent with their basketball family.

Some of the best human beings I have met in my life are current or former managers at Syracuse. They understand that everyone can have influence and add value, no matter your title or role, and truly embrace the meaning of being a great teammate.

SUCCESS STORY:
Principles in Action

> *Good teams become great ones when the members trust each other enough to surrender the "me" for the "we."*
> *—Phil Jackson*

My older brother David implemented a majority of the principles outlined in this book with his seventh-grade travel team when he was their head coach. After watching tryouts with another coach, they discussed their thoughts before making the final decision on the roster. This would be his first time coaching most of these kids, and they didn't know what to expect.

Besides David participating in the scrimmage portion of practices to let his players know he could still ball at twenty-eight, he took an approach the best coaches I studied took: he allowed everyone to have a voice. He was the head coach, but he empowered every single one of his players to speak up, ask questions, and hold each other accountable. He took time before and after practice to talk one on one with his players and check in with them. He emphasized giving high fives, encouraging one another, and sprinting over to help up fallen teammates. He made sure to conclude practice with the accountability circle (principle #14), which provided the players an opportunity to share feedback. He created an environment where everyone felt supported, and things like sprinting back on defense, rebounding, and communicating were praised more than scoring baskets.

David understood if everyone valued things they can control on every play, they would find ways to be competitive in every game. Early on in the season, David realized it was a challenging process to implement this type of culture. However, he was very proud of the progress his team made throughout the season. Like many coaches, he believed his team could be even better the next season now that the *foundation* was in place. In his first season, they went 22–8 and lost in the final four.

Great coaches find ways to evaluate their team's performance after their season. His seventh-grade players would all be moving up to eighth grade and have an opportunity to try out for the team again. David chose to move up with them to continue building the championship culture they tirelessly worked to create that season.

After tryouts for the eighth-grade season, David made the extremely difficult and unpopular decision to cut a few kids who were not buying into the team-first mentality. A few of the kids had been on his seventh-grade travel team the previous year. They were considered by parents and other coaches involved to be very talented players. David received backlash, but he believed he was doing what was best for the team. His coaching the previous year had given him credibility to make these tough decisions. However, determining the final roster was one of the toughest choices David ever had to make because it meant so much to him.

He added kids who brought a willingness to learn, a relentless work ethic, and a positive attitude. His entire roster was a united front. They echoed the calls in warm-ups, the bench was energetic and cheered for each other, and they gave a lot of high fives!

Fast-forward, they went 26–1 and were the number-one-ranked team going into their final-four weekend to compete for the championship. Despite the COVID-19 pandemic preventing everyone from playing the final weekend to determine a champion, the season was a success—not because of their overall record, but because of the memories and camaraderie David helped create for those kids. When playing on sports teams, you don't always remember the records of every season, but you usually remember the memories you created with your team!

David's assistant coach, Brandon, deserved a ton of credit and praise, as well, because he fully committed and cared so much about the kids. He provided new insights while also valuing and reinforcing the exact same things as David. Asking Brandon to coach alongside him proved that surrounding yourself with like-minded, passionate, and genuine people will lead to a positive experience.

Moreover, there were a few behind-the-scenes "extras" that helped make David's team so cohesive, including: team dinners, film sessions the kids wanted to have, extra workouts at the gym that the kids did together, fun basketball homework assignments, and a text-message group they made to stay connected. David also scheduled a trip to a local college basketball game to bond with the kids and teach them. He attended coaching clinics and practices of other teams to learn. Lastly, David made sure to communicate with the parents and get buy-in from everyone associated with the team. This is extremely important, because if parents buy-in, they can reiterate what the coaches teach and will help build a championship culture on and off the court!

I attended a few practices and games throughout the season, and spoke with David before and after most practices and games. I know that the amount of time, detail, and love he gave to his team was given back to him tenfold, and that's really saying something. Players need to know you care about them as people first, players second. David's coaching style allowed him to teach life lessons to his players that will serve them well outside the lines of the basketball court. I consider that the biggest win of all.

Finally, having a team comprised of players who are the "right fit," as opposed to the "most talented," is extremely important. Some consistent qualities of players who contribute to a championship culture include: love of the game, love of competition, playing with heart, positive attitude, staying focused, being mentally tough, communicating, sprinting the floor, talking on defense, boxing out, diving on the floor for a ball, taking a charge, supporting and encouraging teammates, asking questions, being a gym rat, and being willing to do whatever the team needs. Not every player will have all of these qualities, but every player is capable of having some. These qualities need to be praised and reinforced, especially if players lack these qualities but are trying their best to make them a consistent habit.

PLAYERS' SUCCESS STORY:
Take Action

> *What you are as a person is far more important than what you are as a basketball player.*
> *—John Wooden*

If you are currently a player reading this, I applaud you. For you to take time to learn more about culture, teamwork, and leadership shows that you are invested in being the best teammate you can be.

Regardless if your coach values these principles or not, I don't want you to feel discouraged. Energy is contagious, and sometimes it just takes one person to influence a whole team! I challenge you to individually incorporate these principles when you are playing:

- Principle #2: Touches
- Principle #3: Positive Talk
- Principle #7: Point to the Passer
- Principle #8: Help Them Up
- Principle #9: Touch 5
- Principle #11: Next Play
- Principle #12: Bench
- Principle #13: Communication

I'm so excited to be on this journey with you! I'll be cheering for you!

The following chapters are intended for coaches. Feel free to continue reading if you want to learn more about team-building exercises, a sample practice plan, and a culture evaluation worksheet. Please feel free to reach out to me via email if I can be of assistance at: contactdanhorwitz@gmail.com

COACHES' SUCCESS STORY:

Take Action

> *You should pay more attention to how they learn than you do to how you teach.*
> *—Pat Kirwan*

> *A good coach can change a game. A great coach can change a life.*
> *—John Wooden*

Implementing the outlined principles as the foundation of your culture and coaching your players this way may be very different from how players have been coached and how you have coached in the past. Simply reading a book like this shows you truly care about making a positive difference for your team, and you should be proud of that! This is a very progressive, forward-thinking book in showing how to best maximize what you have, rather than doing things the "old-school way" of yelling and implementing conditioning drills to build habits.

Like anything worthwhile in life, you and your team will have to be patient and trust that things will improve. A lot of these principles will be trial and error, but as long as your team is open-minded and willing to try, that's all that matters.

Earl Nightingale said it best: "Never give up on a dream just because of the time it will take to accomplish it. The time will pass anyway." Explaining to your team that the best teams in the country execute these principles consistently will provide credibility and, hopefully, inspire them to buy in.

There will be players who don't think culture is important. However, establishing a relationship with each player early in the season will help eliminate some negative behaviors. Having one-on-one conversations and empowering them are ways to get your players to commit to this culture. Praising the behaviors you expect as often and consistently as possible communicates to those players that you appreciate their conscious efforts. Making specific players—or your whole team—do physical punishments probably isn't the preferred way to get your message across in regard to building a championship culture. It's a waste of time and may temporarily work, but probably won't be sustained in the long term.

Additionally, if a kid refuses to buy in during the season after you communicate to them your expectations, cutting them the following season will probably be the best decision for the team. After all, you want a team full of players who genuinely want to build a championship culture and are motivated to contribute to it every single day.

These fourteen principles will help your team grow both on and off the court. That's why I am excited to hear feedback on how this culture can make a positive difference in a lot of people's lives. Please feel free to reach out to me via email if I can be of assistance at: contactdanhorwitz@gmail.com

COACH RESOURCE:
Team-Building Activities

> *When we perceive differences in personality and abilities as gifts and pieces of a magnificent puzzle, we put them together to form a masterpiece of power and creation truly larger than anyone's single vision.*
> *—Thomas Crum*

Team-building exercises serve as invaluable resources when trying to incorporate a championship culture and team-first mentality. They help develop empathy, strengthen trust, and allow everyone to learn a lot more about the people within their team. As a coach, you need to ask yourself, "Do we invest enough time into having conversations with each other that lead to trust, empathy, and respect for one another?" If a coach chooses to be *intentional* with the time they have with their team, the investment can be extremely beneficial for everyone involved.

In a human-relations class I took during college, my professor made sure to create a safe and confidential space for each of us. She had everyone sign a piece of paper on the first day of class that stated what was said in the room, stayed in the room. Some people refer to this as the "Vegas rule." This is important to mention because adopting such a practice in your own team will help to create the most effective environment to share and grow together.

The other option when you start a team-building session is to allow everyone in the room to call out their desired rules and expectations. For example, your players may say things like, "No judging. Everyone has to be engaged, support each other, be honest, trust each other, and have fun." You will simultaneously write these rules on a poster board that is visible to everyone. The group can then sign that poster board to agree to the rules and expectations. The facilitator can refer back to the "rules" at any time. This is important, and my college professor did an amazing job making everyone feel valued and supported while also guiding the conversations when needed.

Everyone should have the opportunity to share as much or as little personal information as they feel comfortable with. Each individual must know they can choose their level of engagement. Anyone can say "pass" if they don't want to share, and they should never feel pressured to.

The human-relations class took place during the fall semester of my senior year. I learned more about two of my basketball teammates in that class than I did in three seasons of playing with them. The three of us engaged in countless conversations within the basketball context, but none of us felt comfortable being *vulnerable* about our lives outside of the game. That class taught me about the direct correlation between success on the court and bonding off of it. In our senior season, I felt so much more connected to those teammates.

My college professor's empathy, outgoing personality, and kind heart made her someone we all felt we could trust. Once we trusted her, we all worked together to create an environment where we trusted each other. That class added an extra layer of connection among every student and made me feel like we were all family. I think these exercises will have a similar effect on your team.

When you learn about the person beyond the basketball court, you understand that everyone has their own struggles in life. If a player knows a coach genuinely cares about them, they will be willing to work harder and fight harder for them, too.

My best friend and teammate from Newbury College, DaRay, is someone that I would do anything for. We did almost everything together: lifted weights, ate meals, got the same jobs on campus, and shared a lot of laughs and memories. That relationship was built day by day, month by month, and year by year. When he scored in a game, I felt like I scored. When he took a charge, I felt like I took a charge. I understand it's difficult to bond with every teammate, but I hope you can create opportunities on and off the court for your players to develop friendships like this.

Finally, not everyone feels comfortable leading these types of discussions, and it can get emotional. If you coach kids who are younger, selecting exercises that work well with you and your team's comfort level is important. Work your way up to deeper and more meaningful conversations, if the team is willing. At minimum, organizing team-building exercises will show your team that you care about each of them as people and not just as athletes. It will help create an effective environment for everyone to share and grow together.

Feedback sessions after every one of these exercises are extremely important. This is the time where the group can learn a lot about each other. A few examples of open-ended questions to ask after each activity:

- How was that experience for you, and why?
- What did you learn about a teammate that you didn't know before?
- How will this activity help our team improve both on and off the court?
- What were your highs and lows from the activity?
- Would you want to do this activity again? Why or why not?
- Would you want to change or tweak anything about this activity? Why or why not?

SIX BASIC TEAM-BUILDING ACTIVITIES

1. Team Dinner

Everyone can bring something to the house or place where the team dinner is being held. Parents often enjoy taking the lead on this and organizing the event. Families who are willing and able to host usually rotate between their houses, and the players bond off the court in a different, non-competitive setting. If you coach a college team, your program may have enough money in the budget to buy food for everyone. That way, you don't need to have players bring anything. Ultimately, remind your team that this is a time to learn more about all of their teammates in face-to-face interactions, so make an effort to talk with everyone and limit the use of technology.

2. Live Game

Watch a college or professional men's or women's basketball game with your team. This is a great teaching tool to show them what elite-level athletes do on a consistent basis. If you can't all meet in one location, have them all watch the game virtually and take notes at their respective homes. Most Division II and III colleges have a free livestream on their websites, and kids can watch from their laptops or phone. At the next practice, each player can bring in their notes and discuss them with the team.

You can also bring your team to a local high-school, college or professional game, depending on what level you coach. Have your players take notes on whether the teams are exhibiting the fourteen principles outlined in this book.

3. Buddy System

Assign players into groups of two that will be responsible for one another. The purpose of this system is to pair two individuals together to support each other throughout the season. Coaches should be strategic with whom they pair together to best complement one another.

For example, if Kate is frequently late, her partner, Sara, will also be held responsible for her tardiness. Another example is if Sara needs some extra work on her jump shot, she can ask Kate to rebound for her before or after practice.

Having your players hold their buddy accountable and keep an open line of communication will provide a built-in support system that emphasizes the team-first mentality.

4. Causes

What causes are your current players passionate about? Having an honest and open discussion can help bring the team together. Once you discover this information, you can take action and go into the community to support that cause!

For example, my mom brought my brother and I to a "Walk MS" event because someone she worked with had a family member who had MS. When we greeted the family before the walk began, I could see in their eyes the gratitude they felt toward us for participating. The energy and excitement around community-service events are contagious! They also give everyone perspective on hardships that people have to battle every day. The people who are experiencing hardship but choose to remain positive are truly inspiring to be around.

5. Quotes

Everyone can share a quote that means something to them. On a big poster board, each player will write their quote before the activity starts. Then, one by one, they can stand up and read the quote off of the poster and explain what it means to them.

For example, a quote from Mia Hamm: "Somewhere behind the athlete you've become and the hours of practice and the coaches who have pushed you is a little girl who fell in love with the game and never looked back. Play for her."

Having this poster at practices or in the locker room can serve as a reminder to keep everyone motivated. The more we can all flood our environments with motivation, the easier it is to keep going, even when we feel like we can't.

6. What's Your Why?

Learning why your players play the game of basketball is extremely valuable information to know when finding ways to motivate them through the ups and downs of the season. Ask each team member to write down their reason for playing basketball, then go around and ask everyone to share (if they are comfortable).

As a high-school and college athlete, my "why" was that I loved the game of basketball. I loved investing my time and energy into a sport, the camaraderie with teammates, and competing against other teams. I also felt like every time I stepped onto the court, I was representing my family, friends, team, and anyone who helped me along the way. My mom likes the phrase "It takes a village," and I was so grateful to be healthy and physically capable to play the game I loved. My "why" has transitioned into training, coaching, and empowering others through basketball, and I have loved every second of it!

After your players have shared, have them tape their paper up in a place they will see it every day. It can be in their lockers or at their houses, as long as they can read it every day and be reminded of why they do what they do!

FOUR ADVANCED TEAM-BUILDING ACTIVITIES

These exercises are more advanced in regard to the amount of self-disclosure your team may choose to share.

1. Hero

Bring in a picture of someone you consider a hero (alive or not). Share the qualities the person has/had and a story about them. This can get emotional, so make sure to have tissues and have players sit close to each other to be able to put their arm around their teammate and hug them if needed.

2. Show-and-Tell

In this exercise, the person sitting on the chair is the focus of the activity, not an item. One person will sit on a chair or stand up in front of the group. In this five to ten-minute segment, anyone can ask a question to their teammate, coach, or manager. Some people feel more comfortable holding something in their hands, like a basketball, when they speak, so feel free to incorporate something like that!

The questions need to be appropriate and used as a way to learn more about someone's hobbies, funny stories, motivations, triumphs, fears, upbringing, goals, special talents, etc. It's fine for the person to "pass" any question they are not comfortable answering. If conducted the right way, this will build team morale, trust, unity, empathy, and hopefully a lot of laughs!

3. Adversity

> *Be kind, for everyone you meet is fighting a battle you know nothing about.*
> ***—Wendy Mass***

Share this quote, then ask your team to share a time they faced adversity and how they overcame it. This can range from getting a bad grade in class to losing a sports game, or even a tough life experience. If any player is currently going through something difficult and needs some support, the team can help. If it is more serious, then connecting that player with professional resources would be the next step. If the head coach starts off the activity by sharing a story and displaying what it looks and sounds like to be vulnerable, it serves as a powerful experience for your team to witness. Having an honest conversation with your basketball family will help create a stronger bond between team members.

4. Trust Walk

Have your team partner up with someone they think they know the least about. One partner needs to block their vision (either by putting on a blindfold or closing their eyes). Their partner will walk them around in a big space (outside on a field or at a park is preferred, but a basketball gym works, too). The partner who is not blindfolded has to hold on to their partner in some way (hold hands, lock arms, hand on their shoulder) and guide the other around the open area. Try to stay away from other groups. Each team of two can talk about anything they want (make jokes, talk about sports, ask questions, tell stories, etc.). After five or ten minutes, depending on what you feel is best, the partners switch.

I participated in this in my college human-relations class, and my classmates and I were in awe of how well it went!

It's important to have the feedback sessions after each activity to allow everyone an opportunity to speak up and share what they learned.

As mentioned in the beginning of the book, if you are a coach, I challenge you to ask every member of the team these important questions at the end of the season to measure your team's success:

- Did you have fun?
- Did you try your best?
- Did we improve as individuals and as a team?
- Did we challenge each other?
- Did we make each other better?
- Did we create a safe, enjoyable, and hardworking environment?
- Did you feel valued?
- Did you feel empowered to speak up and take ownership of our team?
- Did you learn lessons that you think will serve you well in life, outside of basketball?

If the answer to these questions is yes, the team had a successful season. It's now time for you to write the next chapter: your own championship-culture season!

THANK YOU FOR READING!

If you want to go fast, go alone. If you want to go far, go together.

—African proverb

SAMPLE PRACTICE PLAN

Friday January 10th, 4:00pm-6:00pm

Goals for the Day: Communication, Execution, Energy, and Preparation for Team ABC

- (4:00–4:10) Dynamic warm-up ("**Warm up!"**—echo the call)
- Team huddle at center court with arms around each other
- Quote of the day
- (4:10–4:25) Passing, ball handling, and shooting drills
    - **(Positive Talk, Touches, Communication)**
- (4:25–4:35) Half-court defense and box-out drills
- (4:35–4:55) ABC scouting report with handwritten diagrams of opposing team's plays
- Walk through offensive sets, then defend it full speed
- Walk through BOB (baseline out-of-bounds) and SOB (sideline out-of-bounds), then defend it full speed
- (4:55–5:10) Practice zone offense and press break
    - (**Next-Play**, **Help Them Up**)
- (5:10–5:20) Free-throw groups (**Touch 5**)
- (5:20–5:30) Skill-development groups—guards and forwards/centers
    - Guards: Drive and kick **(Point to the Passer)**
    - Forwards/Centers:
      Post moves, screen/roll and screen/pop
- (5:30–5:50) Scrimmage (**High-Five Line, Huddle, Bench** [subs not in the game], **Time-Outs** [simulate])
- (5:50–6:00) **Accountability Circle**
  (teammates and coaches, positive praise)

If your actions inspire others to dream more, learn more, do more, and become more, you are a leader – John Quincy Adams

CULTURE EVALUATION

For a free PDF template to evaluate your team, send me an email, and I will send it to you (see table).

For Principles #1–5, #12, and #14, you can mark a "+" or "–" **one time** if your team executes the principle.

For Principles #6–11, you can mark a "✓" for every time there was an opportunity to execute the action, then a "+" if your team did, or a "–" if they did not.

For Principle #13, you can evaluate the three interactions (player-to-player, coach-to-player, coach-to-referee) throughout the game and decide how to mark it.

Watching film after a game is a great way to use this chart and evaluate your team. This will definitely help enhance your championship culture. If you have the ability to cut up highlights showing these principles, it will teach your team the expected behaviors of your culture.

Culture Principles	Your Team
1. Warm-Up and Stretching	
2. Touches	
3. Positive Talk	
4. High-Five Line	
5. Pregame Gratitude	
6. Huddle	
7. Point to the Passer	
8. Help Them Up	
9. Touch 5	
10. Time-Outs	
11. Next-Play	
12. Bench	
13. Communication	
14. Accountability Circle (Post-Game)	

MY TEAM—THANK YOU

> *One of my best moves is to surround myself with friends who, instead of asking, "Why?" are quick to say, "Why not?" That attitude is contagious.*
> ***—Oprah Winfrey***

> *Nothing of me is original. I am the combined effort of everyone I've ever known.*
> ***— Chuck Palahniuk***

> *Family is not an important thing. It's everything.*
> ***—Michael J. Fox***

Thank you for being the best teammates I could have asked for on this journey of life. Every single one of you came into my life at some point and brought joy, kindness, and positivity into it. I am forever grateful.

My family: Richard Horwitz, Bonni Horwitz, Sara Horwitz, David Horwitz, Ben Horwitz, Arthur Lapp, Rita Lapp, and Storm Horwitz (our dog)

Rich Forgetta, Felipe Guajardo, Jessica Navarro, Carly Schwartz

Ghamo family: Allison, Joe, Max, Joey, Sam, Lana, Tony, Ileana, Michael, Sal

House family: Dennis, Kara, Julian, Helena

DeCandido family: Mike and Erica

Big brothers: Zach Markowitz, Colin Sitarz, Nick Winn, and Jon Sundstrom

Newbury family: Joanne Silver, Roz Abukasis, Linda Zaitchik, Danny Borrero, Lindsay Graham, Jelani Townsell, Ernest Hughes, Albert Hayle, Alex Schofield, Jenn Forry, Debbie Mael, Avi Tsapira, Stephany George, Katie Collins, Mark Thomas, Andrew Lafrenz, President Chillo, Anne-Marie Kenney, Laurie Gordy, Sharon Roberts, Reggie Williams, Evelyn, Nick, Della, Victor, and my teammates!

DaRay Ross, Bilal NKosi, Rashid NKosi, Prince Boateng, Osvald Duvelson, Jeff Maizes, Sam Linabury, James Hara, Wes Johnson, Cam Van Allen, Kelly Bucholz Smallbeck, Sarah Hope, Katelynne Bazile, Julia Leggett, Destiny Spears, Shelby Gravel, Mark Corey, Matt Gionfriddo, Pat Herlihy, Nico Paruda, Katie Kolinski, Alex Kline, Jake Rosen, Amanda Casale, Brad Scammel, Ryan Beaury, Ricky Pasternak, Chris Henderson, Athan Katsantonis, Brad Pike, Ryan Cabiles, Kelly Seubert, Syracuse MBB Administrative and Coaching Staff, Mike Nilson, Trevor Ray, Brittany Champagne, Liz Cusato, Hailey Anthony, Eric Fluty, Colleen Ames, Trevor Purcell, Jess Mushel, Sam Howe, Matt Dembinsky, Chris Lyn, Steve Philips, Betsy Cohen, Sal Morales, Jake Kelfer, Mike Freilich, Dave Vasquenza, Mike Morhardt, Ryan Aeschliman, Bobby Gerity, Ryan Kadlubowski, Ian Thom, Marissa Robinson, Sharod Williams, Grahm Smith, Brooke Wyckoff, Paul Harris, Billy Clapper, Tobe Carberry, Ken and Maggie Sawada, Mark Walker, Tyler Papadinis, Nick Ciresi, Jay Modi, Bethann Burke, Donny Guerinoni, Mike Donnelly, Bob Sheldon, John Mirabello, Charlie Mason, Mike Pallazi, Brian Rice, Jaquan Greaux, Brandon Hebert, Rebecca Cashman, Katie DaCosta, Chad Turner, Jeff Billing, Steve Boyle, Becky Ahlgrhen Bedics, Tami Matheny, Molly Grisham, Betsy Butternick,

Alyssa Angurio, Dr. Derek Greenfield, Julie Kirgo, Andrea Travelstead, Jay Demings, Denny Kuiper, and the entire BookLogix team

All of the head coaches of the teams mentioned in this book: Geno Auriemma, Adam Stockwell, James Jones, Jacey Brooks, Jill Pace, Stefan Thompson, Dean Smith, Roy Williams, Jay Wright, Tony Bennett, Landry Kosmalski, Chris Beard, Jared Leghorn, Joe Mantegna

To every teammate I've had the privilege of playing with, thank you.

To every coach who has taken time to answer my questions in person, via text/email, or on the phone, thank you.

To every player I have had the honor of coaching, thank you.

Special shoutout to my hero, Bonni Horwitz, for your love, support, and inspiration. Thanks for being the most selfless, empathetic, and passionate leader I know.

Special shoutout to Ben Horwitz, my twin brother, for helping me write and edit this book. You're the best teammate I have ever had on the court and in my life.

Special shoutout to Sara Horwitz and David Horwitz. You two have always believed in me, encouraged me, and offered to help me out in any way you can.

Special shoutout to Sarah Hope for your willingness to talk, text, and email for hours to share your thoughts and wisdom with me. Your encouragement through this process helped make this happen.

Special shoutout to DaRay Ross, Bilal Nkosi, and Prince Boateng for your daily encouragement and motivation. I am honored to have you all in my life.

Special shoutout to Dennis House and Kara Sundlun. Your knowledge, encouragement, and willingness to connect me with other professionals helped make this happen!

Special shoutout to Mike and Erica DeCandido. You two have shown me what it looks like to truly invest in the success of someone you care about. Having you two in my life opened my eyes to what a championship culture looks like on a daily basis.

Special shoutout to Mark Corey and Matt Gionfriddo. You two are the gold standard for inspiring your teams with love, not fear. Your players know from day one that you truly care about all of them as people first and players second.

Special shoutout to Katelynne Bazile and Julia Leggett for your constant positivity, thoughtfulness, and always finding ways to make me smile and keep my spirits high.

To every parent who trusted me to coach their child and share my passion of being a great teammate paired with skill development, I truly appreciate you.

Lastly, for every bad basketball experience I have had in my life . . . I didn't always know it in that moment, but you contributed to this book more than you know. So, thank you.

I AM GRATEFUL!

ABOUT THE AUTHOR

DAN HORWITZ is a lifelong learner who has a passion for serving others. His team-first mentality has inspired him to help create environments where everyone feels valued and empowered, has a voice, contributes, and has fun! His mission is to positively impact as many people as he possibly can. His interests include playing and coaching basketball, team building, being outdoors, and hanging out with friends and family. He was a four-year NCAA student athlete and captain at Newbury College and three-year collegiate coach. At Newbury, Dan was honored with the scholar-athlete, sportsmanship, school spirit, and emerging leadership awards. The mission of his book is to help educate, energize, and empower players and coaches to help build a championship basketball culture.

You can email Dan at: contactdanhorwitz@gmail.com

For a team order of books, please reach out to Dan via email.

Connect with Dan on social media at: www.danhorwitz.com

Services:
-Team Building Consultant for sports teams and companies
-Motivational Speaker
-College recruiting advisor

If you enjoyed this book, your review on Amazon would be truly appreciated. A few sentences about what the book meant to you and how you plan to apply the principles will help potential readers get a copy!

PLAYERS' NOTES

COACHES' NOTES

PLAYERS' NOTES

COACHES' NOTES

PLAYERS' NOTES

COACHES' NOTES

PLAYERS' NOTES

COACHES' NOTES

Made in the USA
Middletown, DE
22 December 2020